3/8/2020
PAGES
85, 86, 87, 88
MISSING. (DF)

Annabel Karmel

Annabel's Kitchen

My first cookbook

EBURY
PRESS

CONTENTS

INTRODUCTION

Annabel's Kitchen is a delightful world, full of energy, excitement and surprises, where children have fun cooking with me and my quirky helpers.

Jimmy is my often unreliable intern (or trusted kitchen companion) from the South Pole, a calamity-prone, fish-mad penguin who's made his home in my fridge. He's incredibly enthusiastic about food, cookery and everything he does.

Pearl is my right-hand penguin who commutes in on her scooter from the zoo to run the Kitchen, organise the website and deal with everything from ordering ingredients to booking my social engagements. She's confident, organised and reliable – the opposite of Jimmy! I often say I don't know what I'd do without her.

Each week, children come to hang out with me in my kitchen and discover the importance of food and its ingredients. Why don't you join us by cooking some of the delicious recipes in *Annabel's Kitchen?* Read on and I will show you the wonders of cooking and inspire you to make your favourite meals. And, yes, in spite of Jimmy's constant disruptions, we always succeed in making fantastic food. In fact, we have a Yummy Scrummyometer which judges the food for its yumminess – a huge nose has a sniff and lets the children know what level of deliciousness the dish is at.

I'm here with Jimmy and Pearl to take you on a culinary journey of exploration and come up with winning solutions in a fun and light-hearted way, proving that cooking really can be child's play. I love it, Jimmy and Pearl love it – so we're sure you'll love it, too!

NO FISH PLEASE, WE'RE PENGUINS

Even penguins who eat fish all the time don't always like it to look too fishy! These lollipops look fun AND taste lip-smackingly good.

SALMON LOLLIPOPS
with orange maple glaze

YOU WILL NEED

MAKES 8 SKEWERS

Glaze
75 ml (2½ fl oz) fresh orange juice
3 tablespoons maple syrup
2 teaspoons soy sauce
1 teaspoon rice wine vinegar

Lollipops
2 x 150 g (4½ oz) salmon fillets,
   skin removed
8 bamboo skewers soaked in
   water for 30 minutes

1 Put the orange juice, maple syrup, soy sauce and vinegar into a small saucepan. Bring to the boil and boil hard for 2–3 minutes, until syrupy. The bubbles will become quite large in the pan – a sign that you should check how much the glaze has reduced.

2 Pour the mixture into a shallow bowl and leave to cool. Pre-heat the grill. Cut the salmon into 4 pieces each (total 8 pieces) – cut the salmon in half, then each half in half again, lengthways.

3 Toss the salmon in the glaze to coat, then thread the pieces onto skewers. Put on a baking sheet lined with foil and grill for 2 minutes. Turn over and spoon over any glaze left in the bowl. Grill for a further 2–3 minutes, until cooked through. Cool slightly before serving. If you like, you can pour over any syrupy juices that have collected in the foil.

ANNABEL'S KITCHEN

JELLY BOATS

Another thing penguins don't always like is swimming everywhere! These jelly boats are good enough to sail away on, and gobble up once you've arrived at your destination.

YOU WILL NEED

MAKES 16 JELLY BOATS

8 leaves leaf gelatine
300 ml (½ pint) cranberry and raspberry cordial
300 ml (½ pint) water
4 large oranges
Rice paper
Cocktail sticks

The gelatine won't set if the liquid is not hot – make sure it is lukewarm.

1 Soak the gelatine in 250 ml (9 fl oz) of cold water for 5 minutes, until it is soft. Meanwhile, measure the cordial and water into a saucepan and warm it until it is hand-hot (make sure an adult tests this). Squeeze the water from the gelatine leaves and then add them to the warm liquid. Stir until they are dissolved, then leave them to cool completely.

2 Cut the oranges in half using a sharp knife – be careful of little fingers! Separate the flesh from the skin and carefully scrape out the membrane, taking care that you don't pierce the skin.

3 Put the empty orange halves into a muffin tin to keep them steady. Then pour the jelly mixture into the cases. Put them in the fridge for about 6 hours, or leave them there overnight, until they are set.

4 Cut the oranges in half again, to make quarters. Cut triangles out of the rice paper to make little sails and then attach these to the boats using cocktail sticks. Add paper flags for a final touch, if you wish.

CUPCAKES GALORE

Make these delicious cupcakes with me and decorate them to look like animals. They're perfect for parties, or just if you feel like a treat!

ANIMAL CUPCAKES

My all-in-one method for baking cupcakes never fails. For the best results the butter and eggs should be at room temperature.

YOU WILL NEED

MAKES 10 CUPCAKES
125 g (4½ oz) butter or margarine
(at room temperature)
125 g (4½ oz) caster sugar
½ teaspoon lemon zest
2 eggs
125 g (4½ oz) self-raising flour
¼ teaspoon baking powder

Buttercream
100 g (3½ oz) soft unsalted butter
225 g (8 oz) icing sugar, sifted
1 tablespoon milk
½ teaspoon vanilla essence
(Alternatively you can use ready-
prepared buttercream icing or
vanilla and chocolate icing.)

DECORATION

Teddy bear
Chocolate icing
(bought)
Chocolate buttons
Mini chocolate
digestive biscuits
White and red jelly
beans
Black writing icing

Frog
Green food colouring
White chocolate
buttons (resting on
cocktail sticks
pushed into the
cupcake)
Green jelly beans
Green writing icing
White writing icing
Very thin pretzels
(optional)

Pussy cat
Yellow M&Ms
Yellow jelly beans
Black writing icing
Liquorice Allsorts

Piggy
Pink food colouring
Pink marshmallows
Mini candy-coated
chocolate beans
Liquorice Allsorts

Tiger
Yellow food colouring
Liquorice Allsorts
Candy-coated
chocolate beans
(for cake
decorating)
Jelly bean

Bunny
Boudoir/sponge
fingers
Candy-coated
chocolate beans
Jelly beans
Writing icing
Very thin pretzels
(optional)

TIP If you are planning a
party, you can make the
cupcakes up to a month
ahead of time and freeze
them in a plastic box.
Defrost them at room
temperature for about an
hour before icing them.

1 Pre-heat the oven to
180°C/350°F/Gas 4. Line
a muffin tin with 10
paper cases. Put the butter,
sugar, lemon zest, eggs,
flour and baking powder
into the bowl and beat by
hand or using an electric
food mixer, until smooth.

2 Divide the mixture between the paper cases and cook the cakes in the oven for about 20 minutes, or until they are golden and springy to the touch. Remove the tin from the oven and let the cakes cool for a few minutes, before transferring them to a wire rack to cool completely.

3 While the cupcakes are cooling you can prepare the icing. Beat the butter in a large bowl, until it is soft. Add half the icing sugar and beat it until it is smooth. Add the remaining icing sugar, the milk and a few drops of vanilla essence. You can divide the icing into a few bowls and colour it with drops of food colouring.

4 When the cakes are cool, swirl some of the icing on top of them and decorate them to look like animals, using the sweets, writing icing and mini cookies.

TIP For the Frog and Bunny, you can push very thin pretzels into the cake and balance the ears on top.

ON THE BALL

Jimmy teaches the local football team. To keep them fit and strong, he and I came up with this delicious dish. Why not make this before heading off to the park? It will give you lots of energy.

MEATBALL PASTA BAKE

You can make as many of these meatballs as you like. Just double the ingredients!

YOU WILL NEED

MAKES 20–24 MEATBALLS

Tomato sauce
2 tablespoons olive oil
2 red onions, sliced
1 clove garlic, crushed
2 teaspoons balsamic vinegar
2 x 400 g (14 oz) tins chopped
    tomatoes
1 tablespoon sundried
    tomato purée
2 teaspoons thyme, chopped
A good pinch of brown sugar

Meatballs
250 g (9 oz) lean minced beef
50 g (2 oz) apple, grated
30 g (1 oz) fresh breadcrumbs
25 g (1 oz) Parmesan
1 egg yolk

250 g (9 oz) fusilli pasta
100 g (3½ oz) Cheddar cheese

1 First make the sauce. Heat the oil in a saucepan. Add the onions and soften for 5 minutes. Add the garlic and vinegar and gently fry for 2–3 minutes. Add the tomatoes, purée, thyme and sugar. Simmer the tomato sauce for 8–10 minutes before adding the meatballs.

TIP To make breadcrumbs ahead of time, whiz a loaf of bread in a food processor and then freeze the crumbs in a plastic bag. You can scoop them out as you need them.

2 Put all the meatball ingredients together in a bowl. Season and mix, using your hands to shape the mixture into 20–24 little balls. Drop them gently into the hot sauce. Cover the pan with a lid and simmer for 15 minutes, until the meatballs are cooked through.

3 Cook the pasta in boiling salted water, according to the packet instructions. Drain and mix it with the tomato sauce. Tip the mixture into an ovenproof dish. Grate over the Cheddar cheese. Place under a hot grill for 3–5 minutes to brown the cheese.

FOOTBALL BOOT BAGUETTE
and football sandwich

After running around in the park you'll need a top-up bite. I make this baguette or its sandwich alternative for Jimmy's football team when the match is over.

YOU WILL NEED

For the football boot baguette

MAKES 2

4 tablespoons light mayonnaise
1 spring onion, sliced
3 tablespoons sweetcorn
2 small cooked chicken breasts, shredded
1 small baguette
A little butter or margarine
A few soft lettuce leaves
Pitted black olives
Red pepper, thinly sliced

For the football sandwich

MAKES 1

2 round crusty bread rolls
Margarine or butter
Cos lettuce leaves
Cheese slices
Tomato, sliced
Cucumber, sliced

1 Put the mayonnaise, onion, sweetcorn and chicken into a bowl. Mix and season well.

2 Cut the baguette down the centre on top, removing a circle of crust at one end, and open it out slightly. Spread the inside with some butter or margarine. Arrange the chicken mixture inside.

3 Place the lettuce at the opposite end to the circle, to be the 'tongue' of the boot. Cut the black olives in half and place the baguette on them – to be studs. Thinly slice some more olives to use as eyelets and place them on top of the baguette. Use thin slices and circles of red pepper to make the laces.

For the sandwich

Cut the roll in half and spread with margarine or butter. Arrange some lettuce over the bottom half of the sandwich and then layer up with slices of cheese, tomato and cucumber. Cut out stars from the cheese slices and stick these on the outside of the bun.

TAKE IT AWAY

Some children who come to my kitchen only eat take-aways. I teach them to make the same food, but they say they prefer take-aways! So once, I pretended to order from a Chinese restaurant and Jimmy dressed up as a delivery man. They ate it all in one go!

SWEET AND SOUR CHICKEN

This dish tastes amazing served with pineapple on a bed of rice.

YOU WILL NEED

1 tablespoon sunflower oil
1 large onion, roughly chopped
1 red pepper, deseeded
  and chopped into
  1.5-cm (½-in) pieces
1 teaspoon fresh ginger, grated
2 chicken breasts, skinned
  and chopped into
  2-cm (¾-in) cubes
50 g (2 oz) fresh or tinned
  pineapple, cut into
  1-cm (½-in) cubes

Sauce
1 level tablespoon cornflour
2 tablespoons rice wine vinegar
1 teaspoon brown sugar
4 tablespoons ketchup
1½ tablespoons soy sauce
200 ml (14 fl oz) water

TIP Ginger is very good if you are feeling nauseous. If you rub freshly cut ginger on your wrist it will help to prevent you feeling so sick.

1 First heat the oil in a frying pan and then add the onion and sauté it for 5 minutes. Add the pepper and ginger and sauté them for another 5 minutes over a medium heat. Add the chicken and lightly brown it with the other vegetables.

2 Mix the cornflour with the vinegar in a bowl and stir until it is smooth. Add the remaining sauce ingredients and stir until they are blended.

3 Add the sauce to the pan and stir over the heat until it has thickened. Season and simmer for 10 minutes, until the chicken is thoroughly cooked through. Finally, stir in the pineapple.

CHINESE FRIED RICE

YOU WILL NEED

MAKES 4–6 PORTIONS
200 g (7 oz) rice
2 tablespoons sunflower oil
2 eggs
2 tablespoons soy sauce,
    plus 1 teaspoon for the egg
2 shallots, or 1 banana
    shallot, thinly sliced

1 fat clove garlic, crushed
1 tablespoon soft dark
    brown sugar
¼ red pepper, diced
50 g (2 oz) baby corn,
    cut into discs
100 g (3½ oz) frozen peas

If you want to make a non-veg version of this tasty dish, you can stir in 170 g (6 oz) cooked prawns or chicken with the rice.

TIP You can buy chopsticks joined at the top, making them easier to use. Or try improvising by rolling up some paper and wedging it between the sticks at the top and securing them with a rubber band.

1 Cook the rice according to the packet instructions. Drain and rinse it with cold water and leave to drain again. Allow to cool. Heat 1 tablespoon of oil in a frying pan. Beat the eggs with 1 teaspoon of soy sauce and 1 tablespoon of water. Cook the eggs in the pan and swirl them to make a thin omelette. Cook until it is just set, then flip it over and cook for a few seconds on the other side. Roll it up in the pan like a Swiss roll, then lift it out and put it onto a board before cutting it into thin slices.

3 Add the cooled rice and peas and stir-fry for 3–4 minutes, until the rice is hot and the peas are cooked. Stir in the soy sauce and omelette pieces and serve with extra soy sauce, if you like it.

2 Heat the remaining oil and stir-fry the shallots for 2–3 minutes, until brown. Stir in the garlic, cooking for 1 minute, then the sugar, cooking for 1–2 minutes, until dissolved. Add the pepper and corn and cook for 3–4 minutes, until starting to soften.

MARATHON PENGUIN

Pearl is training Jimmy for the Penguin Marathon. Last year he came third – impressive, but there were only four penguins in the race. So Pearl has him lifting broccoli to build up his muscles, and I made him this high-energy smoothie and tasty tagliatelle.

RASPBERRY AND BANANA SMOOTHIE

YOU WILL NEED

MAKES 1 GLASS

1 small banana, cut into large cubes (these can be frozen)
50 g (2 oz) raspberries
50 g (2 oz) strawberries, hulled and halved or quartered
3 tablespoons raspberry yoghurt
1–2 teaspoons honey, or to taste

TIP A fun way to eat raspberries is to put one on the end of each finger.

Pearl made Jimmy a 'Winner's Smoothie' – a mix of raw egg, cabbage, sausages and cod liver oil, yuck! Jimmy said he doesn't want to win that badly... Instead I made him a raspberry and banana smoothie (which didn't glow in the dark like Pearl's!).

1 Blend the banana,
raspberries, strawberries
and yoghurt together in
an electric blender.

2 Add some honey to
taste, and stir it in.
It's as easy as that!

CHICKEN AND BROCCOLI TAGLIATELLE

Penguin marathons are just 26 metres, but that's a long way for a Penguin who waddles. Jimmy tried building his own running machine but it went too fast and he somersaulted backwards onto the floor! All the running means he worked up an appetite, but this tagliatelle soon filled him up.

YOU WILL NEED

MAKES 6 PORTIONS

30 g (1 oz) butter
1 leek, finely sliced
1 clove garlic, crushed
150 g (5½ oz) chicken breast,
   cut into bite-sized pieces
50 g (2 oz) button mushrooms,
   sliced
150 ml (¼ pint) chicken stock
2–3 tablespoons double cream
30 g (1 oz) Parmesan, grated
150 g (5½ oz) tagliatelle
150 g (5½ oz) broccoli florets
2 tablespoons chives, chopped

1 Melt the butter in a frying pan. Add the leek and gently soften for 5–6 minutes. Add the garlic and chicken and fry for just a minute.

2 Add the mushrooms, then the chicken stock. Bring the mixture to the boil, then simmer until the liquid has reduced a little. Add the cream and Parmesan and stir until it has thickened slightly, then remove it from the heat.

3 Cook the tagliatelle according to the packet instructions. Add the broccoli to the pan 3 minutes before the end of cooking. Drain, and add the pasta and broccoli to the sauce, along with the chives, and toss together. Serve straight away.

PASTA PERFETTO

When Jimmy returned from a holiday in Italy, he brought me back a pasta-maker. He doesn't know how to use it, but thankfully I do. Follow my instructions and make your own pasta... Once you've made it you can make the ravioli overleaf.

FRESH PASTA

YOU WILL NEED

MAKES 6 PORTIONS

300 g (10½ oz) '00' flour,
    plus extra for dusting
3 large eggs
1 teaspoon salt
1 tablespoon olive oil

1 Measure the flour, eggs, salt and oil into a bowl. Mix it together with a spoon. Then knead it in the bowl, using your hands, to form a dough.

TIP You can make pasta dough a day ahead of using it, or you can freeze it.

2 Tip the mixture out onto a floured work surface and knead it for 10 minutes until it is shiny and smooth. (You can make the dough and knead it in a Kitchen Aid instead of kneading it by hand, if you like.)

3 Wrap the dough in clingfilm and let it rest for 10 minutes at room temperature.

4 Divide the dough into 4 balls. Roll out 1 ball to make a small rectangle using a rolling pin, then feed it through a pasta machine, starting on the widest setting. Sprinkle flour over the sheets.

5 Cut the long sheets of pasta in half so you have two sheets that measure about 30 x 10 cm. Repeat with the remaining balls until you have 8 sheets. Leave to rest for 10 minutes. Toss in flour, then place on a baking sheet dusted with a little flour. Cover with clingfilm if needed.

RAVIOLI WITH HAM AND CHEESE IN A TOMATO SAUCE

If you have never made pasta before, you will be surprised how easy it is and how much fun. There are lots of different ways to make ravioli. You can space the filling evenly in small mounds on a sheet of pasta, then cover it with another sheet and cut round it with a pastry cutter, knife or pizza wheel. Or use a ravioli press – you lay out a sheet of pasta, add the filling, fold it and then clamp down to produce the sealed ravioli.

YOU WILL NEED

MAKES 24 SQUARES
1 quantity of pasta dough
  (see page 28)
flour, for dusting

To make the filling
75 g (3 oz) Gruyère cheese,
  grated
50 g (2 oz) full-fat
  Philadelphia cheese
25 g (1 oz) Parmesan, grated

3 spring onions, finely
  chopped
1 egg yolk
50g ham, finely chopped

To make the tomato sauce
1 tablespoon olive oil
1 small onion, finely
  chopped
1 clove garlic, crushed
1 x 400 g (14 oz) tin chopped
  tomatoes
100 ml (3½ fl oz) water
Dash of sugar

1 To make the filling, mix all the filling ingredients in a bowl and season well.

2 Spoon about 6 teaspoons of filling, keeping it evenly spaced, along one sheet of pasta. Brush a little water around the filling and then put another sheet of pasta on top. Now press it down to seal the edges.

3 Cut around the filling to make squares and score the edges with a fork. Or make circular ravioli using a cookie cutter (as shown here). Dust the ravioli with flour and leave it on a baking sheet to dry out for 20 minutes. Repeat the process with the remaining dough. Cook the ravioli in boiling salted water for 4–5 minutes. Drain and serve with the sauce.

To make the tomato sauce

Heat the oil in a saucepan. Add the onion and garlic and cook for 5–6 minutes, until soft. Add the tomatoes, water, purée and sugar and season to taste. Bring to the boil, then reduce the heat to medium and cook for 5–10 minutes.

POOR JIMMY

When Jimmy doesn't feel well, I help his friends prepare something nourishing for him. Together they make a delicious fruit smoothie and Jimmy's favourite fish dish – which can make anyone forget they are sick!

MANGO, BANANA AND PASSION FRUIT SMOOTHIE

If you aren't keen on any of the fruits in this smoothie, you can always experiment by substituting your favourites.

YOU WILL NEED

MAKES 450 ML/15 FL OZ

1 large mango, peeled and diced
2 ripe bananas, roughly chopped
150 ml (¼ pint) orange juice
2 passion fruits, peeled

Tip You can tell if passion fruit is ripe – the skin is all wrinkled up.

2 Sieve the passion fruit flesh to remove the seeds. Add the juice to the smoothie and stir. Keep the smoothie in the fridge until you need it.

1 Put the chopped mango and banana into a liquidiser with the orange juice. Whiz until smooth.

JIMMY'S FISH PIE

TIP Mash the potatoes while they are hot – cold mashed potatoes tend to stay lumpy.

YOU WILL NEED

MAKES 4 PORTIONS

350 g (12 oz) potatoes, peeled and cubed
A generous knob of butter
A little milk
30 g (1 oz) Cheddar cheese, grated
30 g (1 oz) butter
1 egg
1 onion, chopped
1 tablespoon white wine vinegar
30 g (1 oz) flour
150 ml (¼ pint) fish stock
150 ml (¼ pint) milk
3 tablespoons Parmesan
3 tablespoons double cream
1 tablespoon fresh dill, chopped
150 g (5½ oz) cod, skinned and cubed
150 g (5½ oz) salmon, skinned and cubed
40 g (1½ oz) frozen peas
1 beaten egg, to glaze
carrots to decorate (optional)

Jimmy recently came down with a case of man flu; one of his favourite dishes is Fish Pie, so I made it for him and he soon forgot he was ill. The cheesy mash makes it extra tasty and it's fun to decorate it with fish cut from carrots.

1 Pre-heat the oven to 200°C/400°F/ Gas 6. Boil the potatoes in boiling salted water. Drain and mash them with the butter, milk and cheese and season to taste.

2 Melt the butter in a frying pan and sauté the onion for 5–6 minutes, until it is soft. Add the white wine vinegar and boil for 1–2 minutes, until the liquid has evaporated. Stir in the flour to make a roux, stirring continuously.

3 Gradually stir in the fish stock and milk over a medium heat, stirring all the time. Bring to the boil, stirring until it has thickened. Remove from the heat and stir in the Parmesan, cream and the chopped dill. Season to taste.

4 Divide the fish and peas between 2 or 4 oval-shaped ovenproof dishes and pour over the sauce. Cover with the mashed potato. Brush the potato topping with a little beaten egg. Bake for 20 minutes, then finish off under a pre-heated grill for a few minutes, until it is golden. Decorate with some fish-shaped carrot pieces to serve, if you wish.

PRIZE POTATO

To show the children that potatoes do not have to be boring, I made some animal sculptures out of them, which Pearl even used in an art competition. They look that good!

YOU WILL NEED

MAKES 1 POTATO CAT
1 large baking potato
1 small baking potato
Knob of butter
3 tablespoons milk
25 g (1 oz) Cheddar cheese, grated
2 tablespoons chives, chopped

To decorate the cat
2 cloves
1 plump raisin or a halved black olive
Squeezy cheese (for assembling the cat)
3 long chives
10 g (¼ oz) Cheddar cheese
¼ red pepper
1 green part of a spring onion

Additional decoration if making mouse
Radish, sliced

BAKED POTATO CAT AND MOUSE

This delightful baked potato cat and mouse make a fantastic fun meal.

TIP Prick potatoes with a fork before you bake them to prevent them bursting. You can speed up baking time by cooking them in the microwave first and then finishing them off in the oven to crisp them up.

1 Prick the potatoes with a fork and cook in the microwave for 8–10 minutes or in the oven pre-heated to 200°C/400°F/Gas 6 for 1 hour, until soft. Leave to cool.

2 When cool, scoop out the flesh, leaving a border so that both potatoes keep their shape. Mash the potato flesh and mix with the butter, milk, half of the Cheddar cheese and the chopped chives. Season and spoon the mixture back into the potato skins. Sprinkle over the remaining cheese.

3 Pre-heat the grill to the highest setting, then grill both potatoes for 2–3 minutes, until they are lightly golden and the cheese is bubbling. Put the small potato on top of the large one to make the cat's face. Stick the two cloves into the middle of the face to make the eyes.

4 Stick the raisin/halved black olive nose on using a cocktail stick, snip the chives in half and wedge them as whiskers behind it. You can also use any leftover mash to help stick them on.

5 Cut little triangles of Cheddar cheese and red pepper and stick them on top of the head to make the ears. Attach the spring onion to the back of the cat and pull it round to the front to make its tail. To make the mouse use the raisins/olives and chives as you did with the cat, but use slices of radish for the ears. Make sure you take the cocktail sticks out before eating!

CHICKEN BURGERS

I came up with this idea for making delicious chicken burgers into characters with wacky mashed-potato hair. Cook them with me to make your own burgers with a twist!

YOU WILL NEED

MAKES 6 BURGERS

2 tablespoons olive oil
1 red onion, finely chopped
1 clove garlic, crushed
300 g (10½ oz) minced chicken
Half an apple, grated
25 g (1 oz) Parmesan, finely grated
50 g (2 oz) fresh breadcrumbs
4 sage leaves, chopped
1 egg yolk
250 g (9 oz) potatoes, peeled and diced
4 tablespoons milk
A knob of butter
Vegetables for decoration, such as carrots, peas, red peppers and spring onions

1 Heat half the oil in a saucepan. Add the onion, Sauté for 8 minutes until soft. Add the garlic and fry for one minute. Leave to cool. Pre-heat the oven to 200°C/400°F/Gas 6. Put the chicken, apple, Parmesan, breadcrumbs, sage, cold onion mixture and egg yolk into a mixing bowl. Stir until the mixture comes together and season to taste.

2 Shape the mixture into 6 burgers using your hands.

3 Heat the remaining oil in a frying pan. Fry the burgers until golden on both sides, then transfer them to a baking sheet. Cook in the oven for 10–12 minutes, until cooked through.

TIP Adding apple to the burgers adds hidden sweetness.

4 Meanwhile, to make the mashed potato for the hair, put the potatoes in a pan of cold water. Bring to the boil and cook them until they are soft. Drain. Heat the milk and butter in the saucepan. Add the potatoes and mash them until they are smooth. Season to taste. Fill a piping bag with the mashed potato and pipe the potato around the burgers to create the hair and decorate with faces made from vegetables.

EAT MORE VEG, DAD

One thing I hear time and again in my kitchen is children complaining about their dads not eating their vegetables. So I came up with a plan to sneak those veggies into food without anyone knowing they're there!

HIDDEN VEGETABLE BOLOGNESE

This dish makes a tasty meal for the whole family. The apple is an unusual ingredient, but it adds a hint of sweetness that children tend to like. Serve with spaghetti or rice, or you can top it with a mix of mashed potato and carrot to make delicious mini cottage pies.

YOU WILL NEED

MAKES 4–6 PORTIONS

1 tablespoon olive oil
1 small onion, finely chopped
1 small leek, thinly sliced
½ stick celery, diced
¼ small red pepper, diced
1 small carrot, peeled and grated
50 g (2 oz) button mushrooms, diced
½ eating apple, peeled and grated
1 clove garlic, crushed
1 x 400 g (14 oz) tin chopped tomatoes
450 g (1 lb) minced beef
4 tablespoons tomato purée
2 tablespoons tomato ketchup
250 ml (9 fl oz) beef stock
¼ teaspoon dried oregano

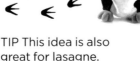

TIP This idea is also great for lasagne.

1 Heat the oil in a large frying pan and sauté the vegetables, apple and garlic for 10 minutes until soft. Transfer them to a blender and add the tomatoes before whizzing until the mixture is smooth.

2 Wipe out the pan with a piece of kitchen paper, then add the mince and fry over a medium–high heat. Break the mince up with a wooden spoon or spatula and carry on until it is browned (you may need to do this in two batches). If your child likes a finer texture you can transfer the browned mince to the food processor and whiz for a few seconds.

3 Add the sauce to the mince and stir in the tomato purée, ketchup, stock and oregano. Bring to a simmer and cook for 40–45 minutes, until the sauce is thick. Season to taste and serve with pasta, if you like.

BEETROOT CHOCOLATE CAKE

TIP Make sure your chocolate doesn't get too hot when you are melting it, or it might turn lumpy. Melt it in a heatproof bowl over a pan of simmering water.

This is such a beautiful-looking cake, no one would ever guess that the main ingredient is beetroot. The great thing about beetroot is that even though it is a vegetable, it tastes sweet, so you can use it to give desserts a healthy boost.

YOU WILL NEED

MAKES 8 PORTIONS

Cake

100 g (3½ oz) Bournville chocolate
125 g (4½ oz) butter, softened
225 g (8 oz) light muscovado sugar
3 eggs
25 g (1 oz) cocoa powder
225 g (8 oz) self-raising flour
½ teaspoon baking powder
½ teaspoon bicarbonate of soda
¼ teaspoon salt
250 g (9 oz) cooked beetroot, grated

Icing

100 g softened butter
100 g icing sugar, sieved
100 ml condensed milk
purple/violet colouring

1 Pre-heat the oven to 180°C/350°F/Gas 4. Line the base of a 23-cm (9-in) round springform cake tin and grease well. To make the cake, melt the chocolate in a bowl over a pan of simmering water, until it is runny.

2 Put all the other ingredients, except the beetroot, into a bowl. Mix together, using an electric hand whisk, until it is smooth.

3 Stir in the melted chocolate and grated beetroot. Spoon into the tin and level the top. Bake for 45–50 minutes, until the cake is well risen and coming away from the sides of the tin.

4 Leave the cake to cool, then remove the sides of the tin and place it on a wire rack to cool completely. Cream the butter with the icing sugar, add the condensed milk and combine until creamy and smooth. Mix in drops of food colouring until the icing reaches the desired colour.

PRIVATE EYE PENGUIN

I lost my ring during a bread-making demonstration and Jimmy decided to investigate. After he'd accused a duck of being the thief, my ring turned up where it was least expected: in a delicious teddy bear-shaped bread roll that I'd baked! Don't lose anything in the dough when you're making yours...

CHEESY BREAD ANIMALS

It's great fun to make bread – a bit like messing around with playdough. You can form the dough into round buns or make delicious cheesy animal shapes.

YOU WILL NEED

MAKES 6 ROLLS OR ANIMALS
250 g (9 oz) strong plain flour
Generous pinch salt
½ sachet (½ teaspoon) fast-action dried yeast
½ teaspoon honey
Pinch cayenne pepper
1 teaspoon dried mustard powder
200 ml (7 fl oz) warm water
60 g (2½ oz) mature Cheddar cheese, grated
2 tablespoons Parmesan cheese, freshly grated

To decorate
1 egg, beaten
Sesame seeds
Poppy seeds
Cheddar cheese, grated
Currants

1   Sift the flour and salt into a mixing bowl. Stir in the yeast, honey, cayenne pepper, mustard and just enough of the water to form a soft dough.

2   Transfer to a floured surface and knead lightly for about 5 minutes to make a smooth, pliable dough. Gradually knead the grated cheese into the dough (this will produce a slightly streaky effect).

3   Shape the dough into balls or animal shapes and transfer them to a lined baking sheet. Cover them loosely with a tea towel and leave them to rise in a warm place for about an hour.

4   Brush with beaten egg. If you are making buns, sprinkle the tops with sesame seeds, poppy seeds or grated cheese. Add currants for eyes on the animal shapes. Transfer them to an oven preheated to 200°C/400°F/Gas 6 and bake for 20 minutes, or until golden brown. The undersides should sound hollow when you tap them. Leave on a wire rack to cool.

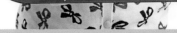

CHALLAH

Challah is a plaited loaf enriched with egg and honey. It's much easier than you might think to make your own and it tastes delicious.

YOU WILL NEED

MAKES 2 CHALLAHS
450g (1 lb) plain flour
50 g (2 oz) caster sugar
1 tablespoon honey
2 eggs
1 sachet fast-action
   (instant) yeast

150 ml (¼ pint) lukewarm water
85 g (3 oz) butter melted
1 teaspoon salt

A little flour for kneading
1 egg beaten with 1 tablespoon
   water
2 tablespoons poppy seeds
   (optional)

2 Remove the dough from the bowl, scraping out any dough clinging to the sides. Place on a floured work surface and knead the dough using the heel of your hand for about 8–10 minutes, until its smooth, shiny and elastic. Alternatively you can knead the dough in an electric mixer with a dough hook for about 4 minutes. Allow the dough to rise.

1 To make the dough, put the flour in a bowl and mix in the sugar, yeast and salt. Whisk together the melted butter, honey and egg and add to the flour along with the water. Mix together to form a soft dough. Mix together first with a spoon and then with your hands. You can put a damp towel under the bowl to prevent it from moving.

TIP There are five stages of bread-making and you can remember them with this sentence: Mary Knits Red Knickers Pretty Badly

Mary = Mixing
Knits = Kneading
Red = Rising
Knickers = Knocking back
Pretty = Proving
Badly = Baking

3 Lightly oil a large bowl and put the dough in the bowl. Cover with clingfilm and allow to rise for 1 ½ to 2 hours until doubled in size. Portion the dough. Once the dough is ready, punch the air out while it's still in the bowl. Then carefully remove the dough, separating it from the sides of the bowl. Sprinkle the work surface with a little flour and knead the dough for a couple of minutes. Shape the dough into one log and let it rest for a few minutes, then cut it into 6 even portions, using a knife. Roll and shape. Roll each piece into long sausage logs about 35 cm (14 in) long. Lay 3 of the logs next to each other on the work surface and join at the bottom. Make sure it is tight but not tight enough to stretch the dough. Repeat with the remaining three. Tuck the ends under and place the two challahs on a baking sheet. Cover with clingfilm and leave to prove until the challahs have doubled in size again (30–40 minutes).

4 Beat together the egg and water, brush over the loaves and sprinkle with the poppy seeds (if you wish). Pre-heat the oven to 200°C/400°F/Gas 6 and bake for 20–25 minutes until well risen and golden brown and the base sounds hollow when tapped.

MIDNIGHT FEAST

From time to time we all get peckish when we should really be in bed. When I had a sleepover with Jimmy, Pearl and their friends, we made a midnight feast – these nachos are the perfect finger-food, but if you've got a sweet tooth, try the Berry Pots on page 50.

NACHOS FOR NIBBLING

I like to whip up some tasty salsa to go with nachos– the crispy nachos topped with scrummy salsa and cheese, are a tasty treat.

YOU WILL NEED

SERVES 4–6

Salsa

3 small tomatoes, deseeded and diced

1 spring onion, chopped

1 teaspoon lime juice

2 tablespoons basil, chopped

a little sugar, to taste

100 g (3½ oz) tortilla crisps

45 g (1½ oz) mozzarella, grated

45 g (1½ oz) Cheddar, grated

1 Mix the tomatoes, spring onion, lime juice and basil in a bowl. Season with salt and pepper. Add a dash of sugar to taste.

2 Pre-heat the grill. Put the tortilla chips in a shallow dish and spoon the salsa over.

3 Sprinkle with the cheeses and grill for 2–3 minutes, until the cheese has just melted. Serve at once.

BERRY POTS WITH WHITE CHOCOLATE SAUCE

A delicious combination of frozen berries with hot white chocolate sauce.

YOU WILL NEED

MAKES 4 GLASSES OR RAMEKINS

100 g (3½ oz) white chocolate
   buttons
100 ml (3½ fl oz) double cream
350 g (12 oz) fresh mixed berries
   (e.g. raspberries, blackberries,
   blueberries, strawberries –
   halved), frozen until solid
2 tablespoons caster sugar
1 tablespoon water

1 Put the chocolate and double cream into a heatproof bowl and place it over a pan of just-simmering water. Stir until it is melted, then set aside.

2 Put half the fruit into a saucepan and then add the sugar and water. Stir over a medium heat for a couple of minutes, until the sugar has dissolved.

3 Remove from the heat and then add the remaining frozen berries to the glass dishes. Pour over the white chocolate sauce and serve.

BREAKFAST FOR ANNABEL

As Jimmy tends to burn the toast when he tries to make breakfast after one of our sleepovers, I like to have some ingredients on hand to make some pancakes, or my favourite granola. They're both so simple and are a great way to start the day.

BREAKFAST PANCAKES

I like to add some fresh fruit as a topping – it gives the pancakes a nice juicy flavour.

YOU WILL NEED

MAKES 8–9 PANCAKES
125 g (4½ oz) self-raising flour
1 egg
125 ml (4 ½ fl oz) milk
4 tablespoons crème fraîche
1 teaspoon vanilla extract
3 tablespoons maple syrup
20 g (1 oz) butter
2 tbsp vegetable oil
Fresh fruit, to serve (optional)

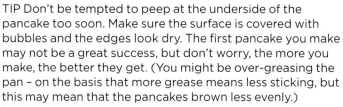

TIP Don't be tempted to peep at the underside of the pancake too soon. Make sure the surface is covered with bubbles and the edges look dry. The first pancake you make may not be a great success, but don't worry, the more you make, the better they get. (You might be over-greasing the pan – on the basis that more grease means less sticking, but this may mean that the pancakes brown less evenly.)

1 Put the flour in a large bowl.
Whisk together the egg, milk,
crème fraîche, vanilla, maple
syrup and a pinch of salt. Add this
mixture to the flour and whisk to
make a batter (there may be a few
small lumps, but don't worry).

2 Melt the butter in a non-stick
frying pan with the oil and
tip it into a small bowl. Mix
1 tablespoon of the melted butter
into the batter. Use the rest to
grease the pan. Drop 2 tablespoons
of batter into the frying pan and
cook the pancake for 2 minutes,
until it is brown underneath
and just set on top (with small
bubbles). Flip over and cook for
a further 1–2 minutes, until it
is golden and cooked through.
Serve immediately with fresh
fruit, if you like.

ANNABEL'S GRANOLA

This delicious granola is very versatile. You can have it for breakfast with milk, but it's also very good on its own as a snack or layered with yoghurt, honey and fruit as a pudding.

YOU WILL NEED

MAKES 6–8 PORTIONS

175 g (6 oz) rolled oats
70 g (2½ oz) coarsely chopped pecans
20 g (¾ oz) shredded/desiccated coconut
¼ teaspoon salt
60 g (2½ oz) soft brown sugar
2 tablespoons sunflower oil, plus extra for greasing
4 tablespoons maple syrup
50 g (2 oz) raisins
25 g (1 oz) cranberries
15 g (½ oz) pumpkin seeds

Breakfast is the most important meal of the day, and wholegrain cereal lke this will provide you with long-lasting energy.

1 Pre-heat the oven to 170°C/340°F/Gas 3. Put the oats, pecans, coconut, salt and brown sugar into a large bowl. Add the oil and maple syrup and mix everything together.

2 Spread out on a lightly oiled baking sheet. Bake for 35–40 minutes, stirring every 10 minutes to break the mixture up into small pieces. The granola should be light golden brown and crisp.

3 After the granola has cooled thoroughly, put it into an airtight storage jar. Add the dried fruits and seeds and mix them in. To serve, put a small amount into a small bowl or ramekin. If you like, layer it in a glass with yoghurt and berry fruits.

PERFECT LUNCHBOX

Jimmy's friends the Cupcakes are hopeless at remembering to pack food in their lunchboxes, though they do remember to pack their make-up and hair curlers! Jimmy just wants to eat mackerel every day. I have to remind them that a healthy diet is a balanced one, so I made this recipe to give them an easy lunch they could make in no time.

ORIENTAL PLUM CHICKEN WRAPS

These chicken wraps are just the right size to pop into your lunchbox, so give them a try. It won't be the last time you do!

YOU WILL NEED

MAKES 12 WRAPS
4 tablespoons light mayonnaise
1 tablespoon plum sauce
4 tortilla wraps
1 cooked chicken breast, sliced
4 spring onions, sliced into strips
¼ small cucumber, thinly sliced into strips

VARIATION
Coronation chicken wrap
MAKES 2 WRAPS/8 PIECES
2 cooked chicken breasts, diced
4 tablespoons light mayonnaise
½ teaspoon curry powder
1 teaspoon mango chutney
1 teaspoon lemon juice
4 baby gem lettuce leaves, shredded
2 tortilla wraps

1 Mix the mayonnaise and plum sauce together. Warm the wraps. Spread mayonnaise mixture along one side. Top with chicken, spring onion and cucumber.

Coronation chicken wrap (variation)

Put the chicken into a bowl. Add the mayonnaise, curry powder, mango chutney and lemon and then mix together and season. Warm 2 tortilla wraps in a microwave for a few seconds. Place them on a board and scatter the lettuce leaves over them. Spread the chicken mixture over the top. Roll up tightly and chill for 20 minutes. When you are ready to eat them, cut the ends off, then slice each wrap into 4 pieces.

2 Roll up, then slice the wraps into 3 pieces on the diagonal.

FABULOUS FLAPJACKS

This is one of my favourite flapjack recipes, stuffed with lots of delicious dried fruit. They are great for slow-releasing energy, so ideal for a picnic snack.

YOU WILL NEED

MAKES ABOUT 15

85 g (3 oz) butter, plus extra
   for greasing
85 g (3 oz) light brown sugar
3 tablespoons maple syrup
110 g (4 oz) porridge oats
30 g (1 oz) Rice Krispies
30 g (1 oz) desiccated coconut
30 g (1 oz) sultanas
30 g (1 oz) dried apricots,
   finely chopped
30 g (1 oz) cranberries

1 Pre-heat the oven to 180°C/350°F/
Gas 4. Line a 20-cm (8-in) square
baking tin with non-stick baking
paper and grease lightly.

TIP When you are lining the tin
with baking paper, leave extra to
come up the sides. This will make
it easier to remove the flapjacks
after baking.

2 Put the butter, sugar, maple syrup and a pinch of salt in a saucepan. Stir until the mixture has melted. Add the oats and Rice Krispies and mix together. Add the remaining ingredients and coat them in the maple syrup mixture.

3 Spoon into the tin. Press down using a spatula to get a level surface. Bake for 20–25 minutes, until lightly golden around the edges. Leave to cool in the tin, then remove and slice into bars or squares.

THE KITCHEN STRIKES BACK

When Jimmy was having some technical problems in the kitchen one day, he discovered that even just getting one appliance to work meant it wasn't a complete kitchen disaster. Together we whipped up this ice cream before his friends arrived. If you're short of time and have friends coming over, give this one a try!

FAR-TOO-EASY BANANA ICE CREAM

This tastes so good and you're not going to believe how easy it is to make.

YOU WILL NEED

4 medium-ripe bananas
Hundreds and thousands

1 Peel the bananas, then place them on a tray that can be put in the freezer. Pop them into the freezer and leave for at least 4 hours or overnight.

2 Once frozen, remove the bananas from the freezer and leave to defrost a little (you can do this one at a time if you want to make just one portion). Cut into chunks and whiz in a food processor until smooth.

3 If you are making the ice cream in bulk, freeze any that is left over in a lidded plastic box. Remove from the freezer and allow to soften before serving. Scoop into individual dishes, then sprinkle with hundreds and thousands.

LIGHTS, CAMERA, JIMMY

Jimmy once decided to make a video of me cooking with a camera his aunt had sent him. Unfortunately, he held the camera the wrong way so all we saw were his beak and eye! Luckily, I had put on food for his premiere, so at least we could enjoy that. If you're having a film night, why not do what I did, and whip together a Caesar salad and some caramel popcorn?

CRUNCHY CARAMEL POPCORN

This is a cinema treat that everyone loves – serve the popcorn in stripey bags or tubs to create the full effect. If you are using microwave popcorn, try to buy the natural, unflavoured type. Yum!

YOU WILL NEED

MAKES 4–6 PORTIONS
Sunflower oil, for greasing
100 g (3½ oz) popping corn or
   1 packet of microwave popcorn
   (natural)
55 g (2 oz) butter
100 g (3½ oz) soft light brown sugar
2 tablespoons golden syrup

1 Pre-heat the oven to 150°C/300°F/Gas 2. Line a large baking sheet with foil and lightly grease it with oil. Pop the corn according to the packet instructions. Transfer to a large bowl and leave to cool slightly. Put the butter, sugar and syrup in a saucepan with 2 tablespoons of water and a pinch of salt. Heat gently, until the butter has melted and the sugar has dissolved, then bring to the boil and remove the syrup from the heat.

2 Let the syrup cool slightly, then drizzle it over the popcorn. Toss the popcorn carefully to coat in the syrup – use salad servers. Spread the popcorn on the prepared baking sheet and bake for 15 minutes. Carefully stir the popcorn and bake for a further 15 minutes, watching closely in the last 5 minutes as the sugar can brown very quickly. Remove the popcorn from the oven and let it cool on the baking sheet for 5 minutes, then transfer it to a bowl and serve warm (check the temperature before serving as the caramel coating can stay hot for a while), or leave it to cool completely (it will crisp up as it cools).

TIP If you are planning ahead for a party, you can make the popcorn the day before and store it overnight in an airtight box. Make sure that the corn is completely cold before you put it in the box; if it is warm it will turn soggy. But hide the box – popcorn is so irresistible that it might not last until the party!

CHICKEN CAESAR SALAD

Caesar salad was invented by Caesar Cardini, who owned a restaurant in Los Angeles. The salad became famous because it was much loved by movie stars in the 1930s and it continues to be a favourite to this day – and children love it, too. Serve this finger-food variation in wraps or small lettuce cups.

YOU WILL NEED

MAKES 4 PORTIONS

2 slices white bread
2 tablespoons sunflower oil
225 g (8 oz) cooked chicken, shredded
8 Little Gem lettuce leaves
25 g (1 oz) Parmesan, finely grated
4 flour tortilla wraps (if you are serving them)

Dressing
1 teaspoon white wine vinegar
Squeeze lemon juice
¼ teaspoon Dijon mustard
4 tablespoons light mayonnaise
5 tablespoons cold water
A few drops Worcestershire sauce
¼ clove garlic, crushed

TIP If you are planning ahead for a party, you can make the croutons a day ahead and store them in an airtight box. You can make the chicken salad a day in advance, too, and store it, covered, in the fridge until you need it.

1 To make the croutons, cut star shapes from the bread using a small star cutter (or trim off the crusts and cut the bread into 1-cm/⅜-in cubes). Heat the oil in a frying pan and sauté the croutons until they are golden. Whisk all the ingredients for the dressing together and season to taste with salt and pepper.

2 Stir the cooked chicken into the dressing to coat.

3 For the cups – divide the chicken salad between the lettuce leaves. Sprinkle each with a little grated Parmesan and a few croutons and serve immediately. Omit croutons from the wrap version. It's fun to roll up each wrap in foil and scrunch one end to seal it. The children can then peel the foil away as they eat, without dripping any dressing.

AT THE ZOO

I love going to the zoo, and Jimmy likes to visit the penguin enclosure to see his relatives. Why not join us having fun at the zoo by making your own train cake, like the one that goes around the zoo, or an aubergine penguin, following these easy steps?

TRAIN CAKE

Keeper Bill who looks after the penguin enclosure and drives the zoo train is retiring, so we decided to make him a train cake ... The beauty of this cake is that it needs no baking, it's simply put together using cakes, cookies and sweets. The children helped me make the train and then we added some gingerbread penguins as the passengers and driver...

YOU WILL NEED

2 Battenberg cakes
11 mini chocolate Swiss rolls
1 tub ready-prepared buttercream
1 French Fancy
1 mini meringue
1 liquorice Catherine wheel
Liquorice Allsorts
8 Oreos
2 oyster wafers or brandy snap baskets
Mini candy-coated chocolate eggs
1 iced doughnut
2 mini gingerbread penguin (see page 112)
Chocolate shells
Iced Gems
Chocolate buttons

For the grass
2 x 250 g bags desiccated coconut
Green food colouring
70 x 40 cm (28 x 16 in) cake board
5 tablespoons strawberry jam
Sugar flowers

For the track
Wafer curls
Sponge fingers for the sleepers

1 To make the grass, pour the coconut into a large freezer bag and mix with a little green food colouring and a few drops of water. Warm the strawberry jam and brush it over the cake board, then sprinkle over the green coconut and press down so that it sticks. Lay out the track by placing the wafer curls in parallel lines and positioning the sponge fingers along them to form the sleepers.

2 Lay out the track by placing the wafer curls in parallel lines and positioning the sponge fingers along them to form the sleepers.

3 Cut off about a quarter of the large Battenburg cake and cut the remaining length in half to form carriages. Arrange 4 or 5 mini Swiss rolls on the track at one end and spread with buttercream. Position the whole Battenberg cake on top. Spread a little buttercream over the top of one end and stick on the cut quarter to form the cab. Finish with an iced French Fancy. Place a mini Battenberg cake piece upright at the front of the engine and secure using buttercream, then position a mini meringue on top. Using a dab of buttercream, place the liquorice Catherine wheel and Liquorice Allsorts at the front of the train. Arrange the Oreos along either side, for wheels.

4 Place two mini Swiss rolls on the track behind the engine and position one of the cut lengths of Battenberg cake on top. Place an oyster wafer on top of the cake and fill with mini candy-coated eggs. Place two more mini Swiss rolls on the track behind the first carriage, and put an iced doughnut on top. Stand a gingerbread penguin on the doughnut. Stick Liquorice Allsorts onto the ends of the Swiss rolls for the wheels. Place another two mini Swiss rolls behind, with the remaining cut length of Battenberg cake on top. On top of this, put an oyster wafer filled with chocolate shells.

5 Decorate the train with Liquorice Allsorts, Iced Gems and chocolate buttons and stand the other gingerbread penguin on the engine. Arrange a few sugar flowers on the cake board.

AUBERGINE PENGUIN

This cheeky penguin table decoration is easily made from an aubergine. Jimmy mistook the one I made for one of his relatives.

Just cut a slice off the base of the aubergine so that it stands flat. Using the point of a sharp knife, trace out the line of the tummy and flippers. Peel off the skin on the tummy and then cut up through the flippers on each side, quite close to the skin. Bend the flippers up a little so that they stick out from the body. Attach a carrot using a cocktail stick to make the nose and two peas for the eyes (you can attach these using a blob of cream cheese). Then add two pieces of mini carrot for the feet. To prevent the aubergine turning brown, squeeze some lemon over the cut surfaces.

ANIMAL TEA PARTY

When I have my special tea party with Jimmy and his friends, it makes it much more fun to have animal-themed food. I love this snake sandwich made from bagels and the pig made out of a watermelon, but you can make your own variations on these party winners!

BAGEL SNAKE

This is a fun way to serve bagels and you can make the snake as long as you like – it all depends on how many bagels you use. It's really quick and easy to make and is great for a special tea party or a birthday party.

YOU WILL NEED

2 bagels

Tuna-salad topping
1 x 200 g (7 oz) tin of tuna in oil (drained)
2 tablespoons tomato ketchup
2 tablespoons crème fraîche or Greek yoghurt
2 spring onions, finely sliced

Egg-salad topping
2–3 hard-boiled eggs (10 minutes)
3 tablespoons mayonnaise
1 tablespoon snipped fresh chives
3 tablespoons salad cress

Decoration
1 stuffed olive, sliced
Strip of sweet pepper
Cherry tomatoes, halved
Chives

TIP If you want to know if an egg is hard-boiled, spin it on a flat surface, place your finger on top of the egg to stop it moving and then take it away immediately. If the egg is raw, it continues to spin.

1 Slice the bagels in half and then cut each half down the centre to form a semi-circle. Then cut the snake's head from one of the pieces of bagel and the tail from another.

2 Arrange the bagel halves to form the snake. Mix the ingredients for the tuna-salad topping and egg-salad topping in separate bowls.

3 Spread half the bagel pieces with tuna and half with egg. Attach the head and tail to the body and use two slices of stuffed olive to form the eyes. Cut a forked tongue from the sweet pepper. Decorate the tuna topping with halved cherry tomatoes and the egg topping with pieces of chives arranged in a crisscross pattern.

PIG WATERMELON

This is a fun way to serve fruit for a party and it's always greeted with squeals of delight.

TIP If you blitz watermelon with a little icing sugar and pour it into ice-lolly moulds, you can make a delicious and refreshing treat.

YOU WILL NEED

1 watermelon
1 cantaloupe melon
1 honeydew melon
Black and white grapes
2 limes
2 glacé cherries
4 raisins

1 First mark out the spiral tail of the pig on the watermelon using a pen or pencil. Cut out a large, round hole from the top of the melon, then cut around the marked-out spiral tail.

2 Use the cut-off top to make a 5-cm (2-in) diameter circle for the pig's snout and 2 triangles for the ears, which you will use to decorate the pig. Set aside.

3 Using a melon-ball scoop, scoop out watermelon balls until the shell is empty. Discard the seeds as you go. Scrape out any remaining melon and drain the shell of juice. Mop up any remaining juice with kitchen paper. Cut the other two melons in half, remove the seeds and scoop out melon balls.

4 To decorate the watermelon, halve the limes and attach with toothpicks to make the pig's trotters. Stick 2 melon seeds into the centre of the snout for nostrils. Push toothpicks into the melon where you want the ears and nose to go, then attach the melon pieces to them. Slice the end off the cherries, push a raisin into the centre of each and attach with toothpicks to create the eyes. Drain any liquid from the melon balls and fill the watermelon with the melon balls and grapes. (Watch if children handle toothpicks – they can be dangerous.)

OINK OINK SANDWICH

A great way to make healthy food look fun!

YOU WILL NEED

MAKES 1 PORTION

1 slice white bread
1 slice cheese
4 currants, to garnish
¼ cucumber
2 slices ham
1 spring onion
1 tbsp cheese spread from a tube
   (for glue)

Cut out the pig's body from the bread using a 9-cm (3½-in) round cookie cutter and two circles using a 5 cm (2 in) cutter. Cut out eyes from the cheese using an icing nozzle. Cut one small bread circle into two, then one half into quarters to make the ears. Shape the remaining bread semi-circle into a snout and cut a piece of ham to fit it and the ears.

Assemble the pig by placing the little circle on top of the large one, and add the ears, snout and eyes. You can use a small blob of cheese spread as glue. Add currants to the eyes and snout. Lastly, finely trim some of the green part of the spring onion to make a curly tail.

CLOWN SANDWICH

YOU WILL NEED

Makes 1 portion
Sliced orange cheese
2 slices brown bread, buttered
Cherry tomatoes and cucumber, to decorate
1 tablespoon cheese spread from a tube
  (for glue)
Carrots, grated with a lemon zester

Place a slice of cheese between the pieces of bread. Cut out eyes from the cheese using small round cookie cutters or the nozzle from a piping bag.

Using a vegetable peeler, take a slice of cucumber and make small irises (for the eyes) using a small cookie cutter. Place the irises on the eyes and position them on the bread. You can use a small blob of cheese spread as glue.

Arrange the grated strands of carrots on the top of the bread and add a cherry tomato nose. If you have small knife, cut a chunk out of the bread to make a cheesy mouth.

PENGUIN NEW YEAR

When Jimmy brought 30 penguins over to celebrate Penguin New Year, everything had to be fish-related. I made delicious Crunchy Salmon Fish Cakes and Fish-shaped Sandwiches. I drew the line at making fish-flavoured cupcakes, but baked some delicious chocolate-orange cupcakes and decorated them to look like goldfish.

GOLDFISH CUPCAKES

These are so much fun to make. If you'd like to try another yummy fishy idea, we also have the fish-shaped Fruity Dip on page 78.

YOU WILL NEED

MAKES 10 CUPCAKES

125 g (4½ oz) butter, at room temperature
125 g (4½ oz) golden caster sugar
110 g (4 oz) self-raising flour
2 ½ tablespoons cocoa powder
2 eggs, lightly beaten
1 teaspoon orange zest, grated
50 g (2 oz) plain chocolate chips
5 tablespoons ready-made buttercream icing

For goldfish
Cheerios
Chocolate buttons
M&Ms (chocolate)
Tube white chocolate writing icing
Jelly beans
Giant chocolate buttons
White chocolate buttons
Marshmallows
Hundreds and thousands
Heart-shaped chocolates

1 Pre-heat the oven to 180°C/350°F/Gas 4. Beat together the butter and sugar until the mixture is fluffy and smooth. Sift together the flour and cocoa powder in a separate bowl. Add the eggs to the creamed butter mixture, a little at a time, adding a tablespoon of the flour mixture with the second egg. Mix in the orange zest and the remaining flour and cocoa, until blended. Finally, stir in the chocolate pieces.

2 Line a large muffin tray with 10 paper cases and fill each one until two-thirds full. Bake the muffins for 20–22 minutes. Allow to cool for a few minutes, then remove the muffins and place on a wire cooling rack.

3 When the cupcakes are cool, spread a little buttercream over each of the cupcakes and then decorate them to look like goldfish.

FRUITY DIP

Sometimes eating lots of fruit can seem pretty dull, but it's not if you have fun with how you lay it out. This fish-shaped fruity dip tricked Jimmy and his penguin pals into getting their five fruit a day without realising it, so why not try it yourself and see how delicious fruit can be!

YOU WILL NEED

225 g (8 oz) cream cheese
100 g (3½ oz) lemon curd
½ teaspoon lemon juice
Zest of ½ lemon, finely grated

Decoration
6 strawberries, thinly sliced
2 slices kiwi fruit
1 blueberry

Fruit kebabs
Use a selection of the following fruit pieces on wooden skewers: melon, strawberries, kiwi, pineapple, grapes, mango, dried apricot, blueberries

1 Beat together the cream cheese, lemon curd, lemon juice and zest. Put the mixture into a bowl and chill for 30 minutes.

2 Decorate with strawberry scales, kiwi fins and a blueberry for an eye.

3 Serve the dip with fruit kebabs. You can make these by threading bite-sized pieces of fruit, such as melon balls, onto thin straws or skewers.

Did you know the more colourful the fruit, the better it is for you?

YOU WILL NEED

MAKES 6 FISHCAKES

250 g (9 oz) cooked mashed potato
   (300 g/10½ oz potatoes)
5 spring onions, finely sliced
250 g (9 oz) salmon fillet, skinned
   and chopped into small pieces
25 g (1 oz) Parmesan cheese,
   finely grated
2 tablespoons mayonnaise
1 tablespoon tomato ketchup
1 tablespoon sweet chilli sauce
1 tablespoon lemon juice
1 heaped tablespoon dill, chopped
25 g (1 oz) fresh white breadcrumbs
2 tablespoons sunflower oil

Crumb coating
100 g (3½ oz) Shredded Wheat
   large or bite-sized
40 g (1½ oz) Parmesan cheese,
   finely grated
2 eggs, beaten

Decoration
Sliced hard-boiled eggs
   (quails' eggs would be good)
Sugarsnap peas
Parsley
Radishes

CRUNCHY SALMON FISHCAKES

You can also make these deliciously moist salmon fishcakes into simple round shapes, but for Penguin New Year everything has to look like a fish! My special crunchy coating is made from crushed Shredded Wheat and Parmesan.

1 Combine the spring onions, potato, salmon, 25 g (1 oz) Parmesan, mayonnaise, ketchup, sweet chilli sauce, lemon juice, dill and breadcrumbs in a bowl. Season well, mix together, and shape into 10 balls. Chill them for at least 1 hour to firm up.

3 Put each ball onto a plate, chopping board or tray and pat into an oval fish shape. Press on extra coating if any bald patches appear. Pinch in the sides at one end to form the tail of the fish. Chill for 3–4 hours or overnight to firm up.

2 Put the Shredded Wheat into a food processor and whiz until you have fine crumbs. Mix in the grated Parmesan. Dip the fish balls in the beaten egg, then coat in the crumb mixture. Dip in egg once again and then coat for a final time in the cheesy Shredded Wheat crumbs.

4 Heat 2 tablespoons of sunflower oil in a frying pan. Fry the fishcakes for 2–3 minutes on both sides until they are golden brown and the salmon is cooked through.

5 Place the fishcakes on a plate and decorate with a slice of boiled egg and the tip of a radish for the eyes, halved sugarsnap pea for the mouth, parsley for the fins and sliced radish for the air bubbles. Serve on a sea of sugarsnap peas.

IN FOR AN INDIAN

To get into the spirit of enjoying Indian food, Jimmy once made a magnificent model of the Taj Mahal out of sugar cubes. This is an easier way to re-create the spirit of India, though – so join me in making these two flavour-packed recipes.

FRUITY CHICKEN KORMA

Here's how you can add ingredients to a curry to make a tasty dish that isn't hot. This chicken korma is smooth, delicious and full of Indian flavours.

YOU WILL NEED

MAKES 4 PORTIONS

1½ tablespoons sunflower oil
1 medium onion, finely chopped
½ red pepper, diced
1 small to medium apple, peeled and finely sliced
2 chicken breasts, sliced into 2-cm (¾-in) cubes
1½ tablespoons korma curry paste
1 teaspoon garam masala
300 ml (½ pint) coconut milk
100 ml (3½ fl oz) chicken stock
1–1½ tablespoons mango chutney
1 tablespoon soy sauce
6 baby corn, sliced on the diagonal
50 g (2 oz) frozen peas
2 teaspoons lime juice or lemon juice
1 teaspoon cornflour

1 Heat the oil in a deep frying pan or wok. Add the onion and red pepper and stir-fry for 3 minutes.

2 Add the apple slices and sauté for 2 minutes. Add the chicken and stir-fry until sealed. Add the curry paste and garam masala, then the coconut milk, stock, mango chutney, soy sauce and baby corn. Bring up to the boil and simmer for 3 minutes.

3 Add the peas and lime or lemon juice and cook for 2–3 minutes. Blend the cornflour with 2 tablespoons of cold water, then add to the curry and stir until slightly thickened.

NAAN BREAD WITH SULTANAS

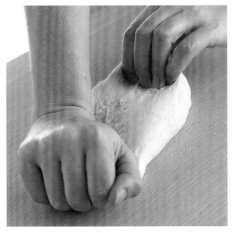

No Indian meal is complete without naan bread, and this recipe is especially delicious as I've added sultanas. It tastes amazing when still warm from the oven, and is good for scooping up any leftover sauce from the curry.

YOU WILL NEED

MAKES 5 SMALL NAAN BREADS

250 g (9 oz) strong white flour

2 teaspoons caster sugar

½ teaspoon salt

1 x 7 g pack dried yeast

150 ml (¼ pint) warm milk

2 tablespoons olive oil, plus extra for greasing

50 g (2 oz) sultanas, finely chopped

A little melted butter

1 Put the flour, sugar, salt and yeast into a mixing bowl. Add the milk and oil and mix together using a wooden spoon until a dough is formed. Tip the dough out onto the work surface and knead for about 8 minutes, until you have a smooth dough.

1 First cook the pasta according to the packet instructions. Meanwhile, to make the tomato and tuna sauce, melt the butter in a saucepan and sauté the onion until it is softened but not coloured. Stir the cornflour into the water, then mix it with the tomato soup in a large measuring jug. Pour this tomato mixture into the saucepan with the sautéed onion.

2 Add the mixed herbs and parsley and cook, stirring, over a low heat for about 3 minutes. Mix in the tuna and heat through. Season with a little freshly grated black pepper.

3 To make the mushroom sauce, fry the onion in the butter until soft, then add the sliced mushrooms and sauté for about 3 minutes. Add the flour and continue stirring the mixture for about a minute. When it's well mixed, gradually add the milk and cook, stirring, until thickened and smooth. Remove from the heat and stir in the cheese. Season to taste.

4 Mix the tomato and tuna sauce with the drained pasta and spoon into a large ovenproof dish. Cover with the cheesy mushroom sauce then sprinkle over the grated Parmesan. Heat through in an oven pre-heated to 180°C/350°F/Gas 4, or microwave, then finish off under a pre-heated grill until lightly golden.

MINI BREAD AND BUTTER PUDDINGS

This is the perfect pudding for when the cupboard is pretty bare. I like to make individual portions in small ovenproof dishes or ramekins.

YOU WILL NEED

MAKES 4 SERVINGS

4 small slices white bread
25 g (1 oz) butter, softened
1 heaped tablespoon apricot jam
50 g (2 oz) sultanas
1 teaspoon vanilla extract
1 egg
150 ml (¼ pint) double cream
100 ml (3½ fl oz) milk
50 g (2 oz) caster sugar
2 tablespoons demerara sugar

TIP Make sure you take the butter out of the fridge to soften it before you use it, otherwise it will be too hard to spread.

1 Pre-heat the oven to 180°C/350°F/Gas 4. Spread one side of the bread with butter, then spread over the jam.

2 Cut off the crusts, then slice each slice of bread into 4 triangles.

3 Arrange the triangles in 4 ramekins or small ovenproof dishes. Scatter over the sultanas. Mix together the egg, vanilla extract, double cream, milk and caster sugar.

4 Pour into a jug, then pour this over the the bread. Sprinkle over the demerara sugar. Leave to stand for 20 minutes. Bake in the oven for 20 minutes, until puffy and lightly golden brown. Serve at once.

ANNABEL'S BURGER KITCHEN

The children who visit me ask for fast food, so I thought up a way to make it healthy. Using fresh ingredients I made yummy burgers with red onion and apple and crispy chicken nuggets.

KRISPIE CHICKEN NUGGETS

I marinate chicken first for my homemade golden chicken nuggets, then coat it in a secret ingredient to make them extra crispy – Rice Krispies!

TIP The best way to crush Rice Krispies is to put them in a ziplock bag and crush them with a rolling pin.

YOU WILL NEED

MAKES 4 PORTIONS

2 chicken breasts (total weight 200 g/7 oz)

100 ml (3½ fl oz) milk, plus 1 tablespoon

1 clove garlic, crushed

1 teaspoon thyme leaves

1 tablespoon lemon juice

45 g (1½ oz) Rice Krispies

30 g (1 oz) Parmesan, grated

1 egg

4 tablespoons plain flour

3–4 tablespoons sunflower oil, for frying

1 Cut the chicken breasts into 1.5-cm (½-in) cubes and put them into a bowl. Mix together the milk, garlic, thyme, lemon juice, ¼ teaspoon salt and some black pepper and pour over the chicken. Cover, refrigerate and leave to marinate for 2 hours, or overnight.

2 Put the Rice Krispies in a plastic bag and crush them with a rolling pin until they are reduced to fine crumbs. Add the cheese, plus salt and pepper to taste. Transfer to a large plate.

3 Whisk the egg in a small bowl with 1 tablespoon of milk. Mix the flour with a little salt and pepper and spread it out on a large plate. Remove the chicken pieces from the marinade, shaking off any excess. Toss in the seasoned flour, then dip in the egg and roll in the Rice Krispie coating. Put the oil in a large non-stick pan over a medium heat and fry the nuggets for 2–3 minutes each side, until golden and crisp and the chicken is cooked through. Drain on kitchen paper and cool slightly before serving.

ANNABEL'S KITCHEN

ANNABEL'S TASTY BURGERS

YOU WILL NEED

MAKES 6 BURGERS

200 g (7 oz) minced pork or chicken
250 g (9 oz) minced beef
50 g (2 oz) white breadcrumbs
1 tablespoon sunflower oil
1 red onion, finely chopped
½ dessert apple, peeled and grated
½ stock cube, crumbled
A few drops Worcestershire sauce
¼ teaspoon garlic purée
2 teaspoons fresh thyme
½ teaspoon Dijon mustard
1 egg yolk
A little oil for cooking
A little Marmite (optional)

These are my favourite burgers, and Jimmy and Pearl are pretty partial to them too! The apple and red onion give it a nice sweet taste with natural flavours.

1 Put the pork or chicken and beef into a mixing bowl and add the breadcrumbs.

2 Heat the oil in a saucepan. Add the onion and cook for 5 minutes. Add the apple and cook for 5 minutes, until soft, then leave to cool. Add the cold onion and apple to the meat with the crumbled stock cube, Worcestershire sauce, garlic purée, thyme, mustard and egg yolk and season well.

3 Shape into 6 burgers. Pre-heat the grill to High. Put the burgers onto a baking sheet.

4 Brush with a little oil – it's quite nice to dot them with a little Marmite, too. Grill for about 8 minutes, turning them halfway through, until brown and cooked through in the middle.

LEFTOVER LUNCH

Jimmy has a naughty habit of throwing away leftovers after parties. I stopped him throwing away some lamb chops just in time once, and made this lamb biryani with them.

LAMB BIRYANI

This is the perfect way to use up leftover roast lamb.

YOU WILL NEED

MAKES 4–6 PORTIONS

225 g (8 oz) basmati rice
150 g (4½ oz) frozen peas
2 tablespoons oil
1 large onion, chopped
1 teaspoon fresh ginger, grated
½ teaspoon garam masala
¼ teaspoon turmeric powder
25 g (1 oz) raisins
25 g (1 oz) butter
1 tablespoon mango chutney
350 g (12 oz) leftover cooked lamb, diced
Flaked almonds (optional)

TIP Turmeric is known as the golden spice of India – add to the rice to give it a yellow colour.

1 Cook the rice in a pan of boiling salted water until tender and add the peas 5 minutes before the end of the cooking time. Drain.

2 Meanwhile, heat the oil in a frying pan and sauté the onion and ginger until soft.

3 Add the spices, raisins, butter, mango chutney and lamb and cook for 4–5 minutes. Stir in the cooked rice and peas and sprinkle with the flaked almonds, if you are using them.

TOMATO AND VEGETABLE SOUP

If you have some vegetables that need to be cooked, why not try this delicious vegetable soup? I just peel, chop and blend all the veggies to make a lovely warm lunch or light dinner. A tasty way to get your 5-a-day.

YOU WILL NEED

MAKES 4 PORTIONS

1 tablespoon olive oil
1 large onion, chopped
2 sticks celery, chopped
1 red pepper, deseeded
  and chopped
1 carrot, grated
1 clove garlic, crushed
1 teaspoon fresh thyme, chopped
1 x 400 g (14 oz) tin chopped
  tomatoes
450 ml (1 lb) chicken or vegetable
  stock
1½ tablespoons tomato purée
Dash of sugar
2 tablespoons double cream

1 Heat the oil in a saucepan. Add the onion, celery, pepper and carrot. Sauté for 5 minutes. Add the garlic and thyme and cook for another 2 minutes.

2 Add the chopped tomatoes, stock, purée and sugar. Season and bring to the boil, cover with a lid and simmer for 10–15 minutes until all the vegetables are tender.

3 Leave to cool for about 5 minutes, then blend until smooth using a hand blender or food processor. Stir in the cream.

ANNABEL'S KITCHEN

PEAK PERFORMANCE

Jimmy joined the local children on the school camping trip as expedition leader, but the children forgot their food, so I offered to help them out with some trail mix cookies I had made – they're a perfect camping snack and slightly more appetising than Jimmy's fish sandwiches!

TRAIL MIX COOKIES

When you go off camping, you need to keep your energy up. This mix of sunflower seeds, raisins, oats and chocolate chips is a delicious snack to keep you going through the day.

YOU WILL NEED

MAKES 18 COOKIES

100 g (3½ oz) butter, softened
100 g (3½ oz) soft, light brown sugar
1 tablespoon golden syrup
1 egg
1 teaspoon vanilla essence
75 g (3 oz) oats
60 g (2½ oz) plain flour
20 g (¾ oz) desiccated coconut
¼ teaspoon bicarbonate of soda
¼ teaspoon salt
75 g (3 oz) raisins
50 g (2 oz) chocolate chips
15 g (½ oz) sunflower seeds

1 Pre-heat the oven to 180°C/350°F/Gas 4. Line 2 baking sheets with baking paper. Cream together the butter, sugar and golden syrup.

2 Beat in the egg and vanilla. Stir together the oats, flour, coconut, bicarbonate of soda and salt, then add to the butter and mix well. Mix in the raisins, chocolate chips and sunflower seeds.

3 Take slightly heaped tablespoonfuls and roll into balls. Put on the prepared baking sheets, spacing them around 7 cm (2¼ in) apart. Flatten slightly and bake for 13–15 minutes or until they are golden around the edges. Leave them to cool on the baking sheets for 15 minutes, then transfer to a wire rack to cool completely.

CORNISH PASTIES

When there was a sudden downpour of rain, Jimmy decided to set up his tent in the kitchen. To cheer everyone up, we made Cornish pasties – as good as a ray of sunshine!

YOU WILL NEED

MAKES 4 PORTIONS

1 tablespoon sunflower oil
250 g (9 oz) lean minced beef
1 large onion, chopped
80 g (3 oz) carrot, finely diced
150 ml (¼ pint) beef stock
1 teaspoon Worcestershire sauce
½ teaspoon tomato purée
½ teaspoon thyme, chopped
75 g (3 oz) cooked potato, diced
2 teaspoons tomato ketchup
40 g (1½ oz) strong Cheddar cheese, grated
250 g (9 oz) frozen puff pastry, defrosted
1 beaten egg, to glaze

1 Pre-heat the oven to 200°C/400°F/ Gas Mark 6. To make the filling, heat the oil in a frying pan. Add the mince and cook over a high heat until browned. Add the onion and carrot and fry for 5 minutes with the beef. Add the stock, Worcestershire sauce, tomato purée and thyme.

2 Cover and simmer gently for 20 minutes, until the beef and vegetables are tender and the liquid has been absorbed. Add the potato, ketchup and 4 tablespoons cold water. Season and leave to cool. Add the Cheddar cheese.

3 Roll out the pastry thinly. Cut 4 x 15-cm (6-in) round circles.

TIP Making a hole in the middle allows the steam to escape during cooking.

4 Put some of the mixture into the middle of one circle. Brush the edges with beaten egg.

5 Bring up the sides and seal at the top, crimping the edges along the top. Brush with more egg. Make a hole in the top of each pastry. Repeat with the remaining filling and circles of pastry (try to make sure you get as much filling as you can into each pastry). Chill, if you have time. Place the pasties on a baking sheet and bake for 10–20 minutes in the preheated oven until golden brown and puffy. Serve warm.

POLAR BEAR'S PICNIC

I asked Jimmy to help me prepare a Teddy Bear's picnic, but he didn't want to come as he had lost Mikey, his trusted Polar Bear. The teddy bear tart I made didn't help – he took one look and sobbed as it reminded him of Mikey. When I opened the picnic basket, guess what I found? Mikey! Now we can all go down to the woods together.

SPANISH TORTILLA BEAR

What better way to have a teddy bears' picnic than by making the food itself into bears? This tortilla looks so adorable you will almost not want to eat it – until you have a bite and see how delicious it is...

YOU WILL NEED

A knob of butter
1 onion, finely sliced
½ small red pepper, diced
100g cooked new potatoes, sliced
A little salt and pepper
4 eggs, beaten
5 tablespoons grated Parmesan
2 tablespoons milk
2 very small cherry tomatoes, plus 1 larger one
2 slices brown bread
A little butter
Sliced Swiss cheese eg: Gruyère
1 spring onion, sliced (optional)

1 Melt the butter in a small omelette pan (20cm diameter). Add the onions and pepper and slowly sauté for 10 to 12 minutes until soft. Add the potato and fry for one minute. Season.

2 Mix the eggs with the milk and Parmesan and pour over the onion mixture. Cook for a few minutes until the tortilla is starting to set around the edges. It's a good idea to lift up the edges once beginning to set and allow the liquid egg to run underneath. Meanwhile, pre-heat the grill. Place the omelette under the grill for 3–5 minutes until golden on top and the middle is set. Tip it out onto a plate.

3 Cut out 3 small round cheese sandwiches using a round cookie cutter, then cut out two smaller circles from two rounds of bread for the ears. Place the remaining cheese sandwich in the middle and place a cherry tomato on top. Add the smaller cherry tomatoes for the eyes and some slices of spring onion on top, if you like.

CHOCOLATE TEDDY BEAR TARTS

I showed Jimmy how to cook and decorate these delightful teddy bear tarts.

YOU WILL NEED

MAKES 4 TARTS

Pastry
100 g (3½ oz) plain flour, plus extra
  for dusting
50 g (2 oz) butter
1 tablespoon caster sugar
1 egg yolk
2 tablespoons cold water

Alternatively, use 250 g (9 oz) bought
shortcrust pastry

Filling
100 g (3 ½ oz) milk chocolate
100 g (3 ½ oz) Bournville chocolate
1 medium banana, thinly sliced
150 ml (¼ pint) double cream

To decorate
12 mini chocolate digestive biscuits
4 glacé cherries
8 almonds
Chocolate chips
Writing icing

1 Pre-heat the oven to 200°C/400°F/Gas 6.
To make the pastry, measure the flour,
butter and caster sugar into a food
processor. Whiz until the mixture looks like
breadcrumbs. Add the egg yolk and water
and whiz until the pastry comes together.
Tip out and roll out very thinly.

2 Line 4 fluted, loose-bottomed tins. Prick the bases and chill for 30 minutes. Line with baking paper and bake blind for 12 minutes. Remove the paper and beans and replace in the oven for 5 minutes until the base is cooked. Leave to cool then remove from the tins.

3 Melt the milk and Bournville chocolate in a bowl over a pan of simmering water until smooth. Slice the banana and arrange in the bases of the cases. Place in the fridge to set for about an hour and a half.

4 Decorate each with two digestive biscuits for the ears and one for the mouth and a glacé cherry for the nose. Finish off with eyes made from almonds and chocolate chips. You can stick the chips onto the almonds with a blob of writing icing.

HOME TO ROOST

This makes a delicious weekend brunch and turns scrambled eggs into a special treat. Sometimes at the end of a long day playing in the park or going to school, all you want to do is sit on the sofa and tuck into some tasty food, and this burrito is so quick to make you'll be on the couch in no time.

BREAKFAST BURRITO

The salsa and sweet pepper and onion mixture can be made ahead, just cover and refrigerate until it is needed. Alternatively, use a bought salsa.

YOU WILL NEED

MAKES 2

Salsa
1 medium-ripe tomato, skinned and deseeded
1 spring onion, thinly sliced
½ red chilli, deseeded (optional)
1 teaspoon lemon juice
Or use 3 tablespoons of your favourite bought salsa

Burrito filling
1 small red onion, thinly sliced
½ red pepper, deseeded and thinly sliced
1 tablespoon sunflower or olive oil
1 teaspoon balsamic vinegar, plus a large pinch of Spanish paprika or pinch of coriander

Scrambled eggs
25 g (1 oz) butter
3 eggs
1 tablespoon chopped coriander (optional)

2 large soft tortilla wraps
Soured cream, to serve (optional)

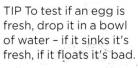

TIP To test if an egg is fresh, drop it in a bowl of water – if it sinks it's fresh, if it floats it's bad.

1 Mix the salsa ingredients together and season with salt and pepper. Set aside. Sauté the onion and pepper in the oil for 10 minutes, or until soft. Add the balsamic vinegar and smoked paprika or coriander and cook for a minute. Set aside to cool slightly while you scramble the eggs.

2 Melt the butter in a frying pan and add the eggs. Cook, stirring until softly scrambled, stir in the coriander (if using) and season to taste with salt and pepper. Warm the tortillas in a microwave for about 10 seconds or in a dry frying pan for about 30 seconds.

3 Warm the pepper mixture in a saucepan or in the microwave for 15–20 seconds. Divide the onion and pepper mixture between the tortillas, keeping it in the centre. Add the eggs, then a spoonful of salsa. Fold the edges in, then roll up the tortilla to make a burrito. If you like, serve them with a little soured cream.

MINI CHEESE SOUFFLÉS

Naughty Jimmy tried to hide his uncle's chicken, Caroline, in the kitchen, but she was giving Pearl the sniffles. Jimmy accidentally dropped one of the eggs I had set aside to make a soufflé, but luckily Caroline laid one just then, so I had three for my soufflé!

TIP To test if the egg whites are stiff enough, hold the bowl over the top of your head. If the eggs don't fall out, then they are stiff enough to use.

YOU WILL NEED

MAKES 4–6

40 g (1½ oz) butter
40 g (1½ oz) plain flour
300 ml (½ pint) whole milk
½ teaspoon Dijon mustard
45 g (1½ oz) Parmesan cheese, finely grated
25 g (1 oz) strong Cheddar cheese, grated
25 g (1 oz) Gruyère, grated
3 large eggs, separated

1 Pre-heat the oven to 220°C/425°F/Gas 7. Put a baking sheet into the oven to heat it up. Lightly grease 4 ramekins with soft butter.

2 Melt the butter in a saucepan and add the flour. Stir over the heat for a few seconds then blend in the milk, whisking until smooth and thickened. Remove from the heat and add the mustard and cheeses. Stir until melted then add the egg yolks. Season.

3 Put the egg whites into a food mixer and whisk until you create stiff peaks. Fold 1 tablespoon of egg whites into the cheese mixture to loosen the consistency, then fold in the remaining egg whites. Spoon into the ramekins.

4 Place the ramekins onto the hot baking sheet and bake until they are well risen (about 12 minutes) and lightly golden on top. Serve at once.

SPRINGTIME

These are Jimmy, Pearl and my favourite recipes to see off the winter cold, and welcome in the spring.

TIP If you heat your spoon in hot water before you measure out the syrup, it will slide off it easily.

ANNABEL'S GINGER COOKIES

These are my favourite ginger cookies and they only take a few minutes to prepare.

YOU WILL NEED

MAKES ABOUT 15 COOKIES, DEPENDING ON YOUR COOKIE CUTTER

185 g (6½ oz) plain flour, plus extra for dusting
1½ teaspoons ground ginger
½ teaspoon bicarbonate of soda
50 g (2 oz) butter, at room temperature
85 g (3 oz) soft, light brown sugar
1 egg yolk
2 tablespoons golden syrup

Assorted decorations
White and pink icing made with Royal Icing mixed with water
Mini candy-coated chocolate beans (used for cake decorating) or mini Smarties
Hundreds and thousands

1 Pre-heat the oven to 180°C/350°F/Gas 4. Line or grease 2 large baking sheets with non-stick baking paper. Sift the flour, ginger and bicarbonate of soda into a mixing bowl. Cut the butter into chunks and add to the bowl.

2 Rub the butter into the flour using your fingers, until the mixture looks like fine breadcrumbs. Stir the sugar into the mixture, then add the egg yolk and golden syrup and mix everything together using a wooden spoon.

3 Sprinkle a clean work surface with flour and knead the dough until it is smooth. Cut the dough in half. Sprinkle the work surface with a little more flour and roll out the dough, starting at the centre and rolling outwards evenly. Repeat with the second ball of dough.

4 Cut into shapes using cookie cutters. Re-roll the trimmings until you have used up all the dough. Place on the lined or greased baking sheets and bake for 10–12 minutes. You can add currants for eyes before the cookies are baked, if you like. Allow to cool, then transfer to a wire rack to cool completely. Once cool, decorate with chocolate beans or mini Smarties, or hundreds and thousands, and pipe on the icing.

ANNABEL'S VEGGIE BURGERS

These are very popular in my house and even confirmed veggie-haters seem to like them. If you want to freeze these burgers it's best to do so when they have been cooked. Just place them on a tray lined with clingfilm and when they are frozen, wrap them individually in clingfilm. You can then remove them and use as many as you like at a time. You can serve the burgers in buns and decorate them to look like rabbits.

YOU WILL NEED

MAKES 8 BURGERS

350 g (12 oz) medium potatoes,
 with skins on
1½ tablespoons olive oil
150 g (5½ oz) red onion, finely chopped
150 g (5½ oz) small leek, chopped
150 g (5½ oz) carrot, grated
100 g (3½ oz) brown cap mushrooms,
 diced
1 clove garlic, crushed
1 teaspoon fresh thyme leaves
1 tablespoon soy sauce
40 g (1½ oz) Gruyère cheese, grated
75 g (3 oz) fresh breadcrumbs
2 teaspoons clear honey
1 small egg yolk
Flour, for dusting
Sunflower oil, for frying
8 bread rolls, tomato ketchup
 and salad, to serve
Cucumber and cheese slices,
 to decorate (optional)

1 Prick the potatoes. Cook them in the microwave for about 10 minutes, until soft. Alternatively, boil the potatoes in a pan of water for 30 minutes with the skins on. Set aside to cool.

2 Meanwhile, heat the olive oil in a large frying pan and sauté the onion, leek, carrot, mushrooms, garlic and thyme for 10 minutes, stirring occasionally until the vegetables are soft. Make sure the mixture is quite dry and leave to cool down completely.

3 Peel the potatoes and lightly mash with a fork. Add the cold vegetables and remaining ingredients, except for the oil and flour. Mix together and season well.

4 Shape into 8 burgers, set aside in the fridge for 30 minutes. Lightly flour both sides, then fry in a little sunflower oil for about 3–4 minutes on each side until golden and cooked through. Serve in a bun with salad and ketchup. If you like, cut some ears, eyes and a nose out of cheese and cucumber.

EASTER CAKES

I love to make these delicious Easter cakes with marzipan and fruit, and decorate them with baby chicks. You can add any chocolate eggs the Easter Bunny might have brought you, like Jimmy does.

YOU WILL NEED

MAKES 12

150 g (5½ oz) butter, softened
150 g (5½ oz) caster sugar
2 large eggs
150 g (5½ oz) self-raising flour
½ teaspoon baking powder
1 teaspoon ground cinnamon
1 teaspoon mixed spice
50 g (2 oz) peeled apple, grated
25 g (1 oz) dried apricots,
    chopped finely
25 g (1 oz) sultanas
25 g (1 oz) golden marzipan, grated

Icing
100 g (3½ oz) butter, softened
100 g (3½ oz) icing sugar, sifted
50 g (2 oz) cream cheese

Decoration
Yellow fondant or marzipan
    for the chick
Black writing icing for the eyes
Mini Easter eggs

1 Pre-heat the oven to 180°C/350°F/Gas 4. Line a muffin tin with paper cases. Put the butter, caster sugar, eggs, flour and baking powder into a mixing bowl and beat together by hand or using an electric mixer.

2 Add the remaining ingredients and beat again. Spoon into the paper cases. Bake for 20–25 minutes until lightly golden and well risen. Leave to cool on a wire rack.

3 To make the icing, beat all of the icing ingredients together until smooth. Spread onto the cold cupcakes. Mould the fondant or marzipan into the shape of a chick, draw on some black eyes using writing icing and add a couple of mini Easter eggs.

FOOD IN A FLASK

Sometimes when you're outside you want something warming to eat that's easy to carry around. This chowder tastes so good, and you can fill up the flask with it so you can have more than one serving. The pitta goes nicely with it.

CHICKEN AND CORN CHOWDER

This soup is very quick to prepare and is a complete meal in one bowl. It's great to include in a lunchbox flask when the weather gets cold.

YOU WILL NEED

MAKES 4 PORTIONS

15 g (½ oz) butter
2 large shallots, finely chopped
1 medium potato, peeled and diced into 1-cm (⅜-in) cubes
1 x 400 g (14 oz) tin sweetcorn, drained
600 ml (1 pint) good chicken or vegetable stock
6 tablespoons double cream
75 g (3 oz) cooked, shredded chicken
1 tablespoon chopped parsley (optional), to serve

MAKES 4 HALVES PITTA POCKETS

2 pitta breads
4 tablespoons hummus
1 carrot
50 g (2 oz) Cheddar cheese, grated
¼ cucumber, sliced
1 teaspoon lemon juice

1 Melt the butter in a large saucepan and sauté the shallots for 5 minutes, until soft. Add the potato, corn and stock, bring to a simmer and cook until the potato is soft. Blend half of this mixture until smooth, then return to the pan and stir in the double cream. Season to taste.

2 Stir in the shredded chicken. Serve with a little chopped parsley scattered over, if you like.

To make the pitta

Warm the pitta breads (but not if you are using them in a lunchbox), then slice each one in half widthways. Open them up and spread a tablespoon of hummus on one side and fill with grated carrots, grated cheese and cucumber. Squeeze over a little

WORLD RECORD

Jimmy is determined to get into the Penguin Book of Records. His first attempt – the World's Biggest Pizza – was a disaster, so I suggested something easier – the World's Smallest Breakfast. Together we made Quail's Eggs on Tiny Toasts, but Pearl said there was a penguin in Texas who holds the record for a flea egg omelette. To cheer Jimmy up, we made him his all-time favourite recipe – 'Granny Plankton's Salmon Surprise' – a dish that should win the Yummiest Recipe Ever.

SALMON SURPRISE

Make one large salmon in pastry or small individual ones. It's fun to shape the pastry like a fish and much easier than you think!

YOU WILL NEED

MAKES 6 PORTIONS

2 x 350 g (12 oz) pieces of salmon tail fillet, skinned and pinned

Filling
200 g (7 oz) baby spinach
150 g (4½ oz) ricotta cheese
50 g (2 oz) Parmesan cheese, grated
1 egg yolk
Pinch ground nutmeg
4 spring onions, finely sliced
1 x 500 g (1 lb 1 oz) block puff pastry
1 egg, beaten

Sauce
1 teaspoon oil
1 onion, finely diced
1 teaspoon white wine vinegar
100 ml (3½ fl oz) fish stock
100 ml (3½ fl oz) double cream
Dash lemon juice
2 teaspoons chives, snipped

1 Pre-heat the oven to 220°C/425°F/Gas 7. Lay the salmon fillets on a board and season with salt and pepper. To make the filling, cook the washed spinach in a large frying pan until wilted. Drain in a colander, squeezing as much liquid out of the spinach as possible. Set aside to cool. Mix the ricotta, Parmesan, egg yolk, nutmeg and spring onions in a bowl. Add the cold spinach and season well.

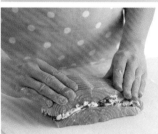

2 Roll two-thirds of the pastry to about 35 cm x 30 cm (14 in x 13 in) rectangle and place one fillet lengthways in the middle. Spread the filling on top of the fillet, then place the other fillet on top so it makes a sort of sandwich.

3 Brush the edges with beaten egg, then fold in the sides to seal, making sure you have quite a bit of overhang at both ends to make the head and tail.

4 Turn the fish upside down onto a baking sheet lined with non-stick paper so the seal is underneath. Tuck the end under to make a rounded head. Snip the other end and shape into a fish tail. Brush with egg. Roll out the remaining pastry and cut out small crescents or semi-circles to make scales. Decorate the body with these and make an eye and mouth out of pastry. Once you've added the decorations, brush the pastry with egg again. Chill, if you have time. Bake for 30–35 minutes until the pastry is golden brown and the salmon is cooked.

5 Heat the oil. Add the onion and simmer for 5 minutes until soft. Next add the vinegar and reduce, then add the stock and reduce by half. Pour in the cream and reduce for 2 minutes. Finally add the lemons, chives and seasoning. Serve with the salmon.

IF I WERE A SCULPTOR

I made these ice lollies when Jimmy's attempts to make a penguin sculpture ended in a big puddle. On a beautiful sunny day, ice cream and ice lollies just have to be on the menu, so why not make them as pretty as a sculpture?

YOU WILL NEED

MAKES 4 LOLLIES

100 ml (3½ fl oz) red grape juice

1 tablespoon icing sugar

100 g (3½ oz) ripe mango, peeled, pitted and diced

2 tablespoons tropical fruit juice

1–2 tablespoons icing sugar (optional)

3 large kiwi fruits, peeled and cut into chunks

3 tablespoons icing sugar

ICE LOLLIES

These delicious three-tiered lollies are wonderfully refreshing on a hot day. Made from mango, kiwi and red grape juice, it's a thirst quencher that everyone can get involved in making.

1 Mix the grape juice and icing sugar together. Pour into lolly moulds and freeze for 1–2 hours until just firm.

2 Blend together the mango and tropical fruit juice in a blender. Taste and add a little icing sugar if needed (it depends how ripe your mango is). Pour into lolly moulds or freezerproof glasses.

3 Freeze for 1–2 hours until just firm. Remove from the freezer, insert lolly sticks and freeze overnight.

4 Purée the kiwis, pushing them through a fine sieve to remove the seeds. Then stir in the icing sugar. You should have 100 ml (3½ fl oz). Pour into lolly moulds and freeze again overnight.

DOUBLE RASPBERRY RIPPLE ICE CREAM

YOU WILL NEED

150 g (¼ pint) good-quality
  raspberry whole-milk
  yoghurt
100 ml (3½ fl oz) double cream
50 g (2 oz) raspberries
2 tablespoons icing sugar

Sauce
100 g (3½ oz) raspberries
½ teaspoon lemon juice
1–2 tablespoons icing sugar,
  or to taste

You can easily double the ingredients to have twice as much tastiness!

1 Blend the ice-cream ingredients together and churn in an ice-cream maker, following the manufacturer's instructions. If you don't have a machine, just stir several times during freezing to break up any ice particles. Next, make the sauce. Purée the raspberries and lemon juice in a blender, then push through a sieve. Stir in the icing sugar, then taste and add extra sugar if needed (depending on the ripeness of the raspberries).

2 When the ice cream is frozen, scoop it into a large plastic container and roughly fold through the sauce so that it ripples through the ice cream. Freeze for 1–2 hours to firm up the sauce. It is best to eat the ice cream within a week.

INDEX

ABOUT THE AUTHOR

Annabel Karmel is the UK's best-selling author on baby and children's food and nutrition. She is an expert in devising tasty and nutritious meals for children without the need for parents to spend hours in the kitchen.

A mother of three, Annabel is the number-one parenting author in the UK and fourth best-selling cookery writer. She has written 22 books on feeding babies and children (as well as teaching children how to cook), including Complete Family Meal Planner, The Fussy Eaters Recipe Book and the Princess Party Cookbook. Her books have sold over 4 million copies worldwide. Her Complete Baby and Toddler Meal Planner has become the authoritative guide on feeding babies and children and is regularly in the top five cookery titles.

Books are not the only string to Annabel's bow; she has created the Eat Fussy range of chilled meals, which is now the number-one range of branded ready meals for children in supermarkets. She has the popular Make it Easy range of equipment for preparing baby food. Annabel has also created a co-branded range of Healthy Foods for young children with Disney, and has developed her own collection of cooking equipment for aspiring junior chefs.

Annabel is passionate about improving the way children eat in popular family attractions, hotels, pubs and restaurants, and her menus can be found in all the major theme parks including Legoland and Thorpe Park, as well the UK's largest Holiday Park group – Haven Holidays and Butlins. In 2009 Annabel won a prestigious Caterer and Hotelkeeper Excellence in Food award for her children's meals, as well as the Lifetime Achievement award at the Mother and Baby Awards in 2009.

Her popular website www.annabelkarmel.com has more than 80,000 members, and offers parents delicious recipes for babies, children and adults, as well as information on all aspects of nutrition.

Annabel writes regularly for national newspapers and magazines and also appears frequently on radio and television as the expert on child nutritional issues, including This Morning, BBC Breakfast, Sky News and Radio 2, 4 and 5 amongst others. She was recently voted as one of the iconic chefs of her generation for ITV's This Morning.

Annabel was awarded an MBE in June 2006 in the Queen's Birthday Honours for her outstanding work in the field of child nutrition.

ACKNOWLEDGEMENTS

I would like to thank the following for their help and work on this book: Dave King for his wonderful photography; Smith & Gilmour for art direction and beautiful design; Liz Thomas for hair and make-up: food stylists Seiko Hatfield and Kate Blinman; Lucinda Kaicik; Richard Fegen, Marina Magpoc; Jo Harris for her props styling; the team at Ebury Press, including Fiona Macintyre, Carey Smith and Hannah Knowles; and Jo Godfrey Wood, Helena Caldon, and Evelyn Etkind. A big thank you to all the lovely children who were involved in the photoshoot: Jordan Anderton, Lottie Evered, Hope Hancock, Tanya Kanani, Tammy Reese, Eliza Wade, and Jude and Sasha Willoughby.

Lastly but by no means least, I would like to thank my children, Nicholas, Lara and Scarlett, for tasting all my recipes.

www.annabelkarmel.com

OTHER TITLES AVAILABLE

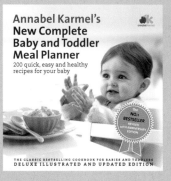

10 9 8 7 6 5 4 3 2

Published in 2011 by Ebury Press, an imprint of Ebury Publishing

Ebury Publishing is a division of the Random House Group

Text © Annabel Karmel 2011
Photography © Dave King 2011

Annabel Karmel has asserted her right to be identified as the author of this Work in accordance with the Copyright, Designs and Patents Act 1988

The Random House Group Limited Reg. No. 954009

Addresses for companies within the Random House Group can be found at www.randomhouse.co.uk

A CIP catalogue record for this book is available from the British Library

The Random House Group Limited makes every effort to ensure that the papers used in our books are made from trees that have been legally sourced from well-managed and credibly certified forests. Our paper procurement policy can be found on www.randomhouse.co.uk/environment

Design: Smith & Gilmour
Printed and bound by Firmengruppe APPL, Wemding, Germany

ISBN 978-0-09-194311-0